ASYMMETRIC PASS-THROUGH IN U.S. GASOLINE PRICES*

Matthew Chesnes[†]

Bureau of Economics
Federal Trade Commission

June 18, 2010

*The opinions expressed here are those of the author and not necessarily those of the Federal Trade Commission or any of its Commissioners. I thank Michael Noel, Matthew Lewis, Chris Taylor, Louis Silvia, David Meyer, Doug Herman, and participants at the 2010 International Industrial Organization Conference for their suggestions and comments. Elisabeth Murphy provided excellent research assistance. All remaining errors are my own.

[†]Email: mchesnes@ftc.gov.

Abstract

This paper presents new evidence of asymmetric pass-through, the notion that upward cost shocks are passed through faster than downward cost shocks, in U.S. gasoline prices. Much of the extant literature comes to seemingly contradictory conclusions about the existence of an asymmetry, though the differences may be due to different aggregation (both over time and geographic markets) and the use of different price series including crude oil, wholesale, and retail gasoline prices. I utilize a large and detailed dataset to determine where evidence of a pass-through asymmetry exists, and how it depends on the aggregation and price series chosen by the researcher.

Using the standard error correction model, I find evidence of pass-through asymmetry in the response of daily and weekly retail prices to wholesale rack price changes, though the magnitude varies by geographic market. On average, retail prices rise more than four times as fast as they fall. Branded gasoline features significantly more asymmetry with respect to rack prices compared with unbranded gasoline. Over time, nation-wide asymmetry varies significantly from year to year peaking in 2005. Midwest cities, like Louisville and Minneapolis, feature more asymmetry compared with other parts of the country. F-tests broadly confirm the results and illustrate that data selection and aggregation, as well as model specification, can have important implications on the findings of asymmetric pass-through.

1   Introduction

There is a large literature analyzing the cost to price pass-through in industries ranging from automobiles (Gron and Swenson (1982)), to cheese products (Kim and Cotterill (2008)), to the beef industry (Goodwin and Holt (1999)). The literature has not only focused on the ability of firms to successfully capture rents when input costs change, but also on how the rate of pass-through varies when the costs increase versus decrease. In the gasoline industry, this asymmetric phenomenon is known as *rockets and feathers*, reflecting the fact that retail prices tend to increase quickly when costs (say, wholesale gasoline prices) rise, but drift down slowly when they fall.[1] Much of the extant literature comes to seemingly contradictory conclusions about the existence of this phenomenon, though the differences may be due to different data sources, price series, aggregation over time and across geographic areas, as well as misspecified models. In this paper, I re-examine the pass-through in gasoline prices using a detailed dataset available at a high frequency, across many cities, and at several price levels in the vertical distribution process for gasoline.

The gasoline industry has been the focus of a particularly large amount of research on pass-through for several reasons. Gasoline is a fairly homogeneous product and both retail and intermediate wholesale prices are relatively transparent compared with other industries.[2] Much of the variation in gasoline prices is driven by the price of crude oil, the key input into gasoline.[3] This crude oil is traded on a world market and the price is also transparent to market players and to consumers. In spite of this, there are

---

[1] The production and distribution of gasoline is just one part of the petroleum industry, which produces a whole range of refined products. The rockets and feathers literature has focused primarily on gasoline prices.

[2] Rack prices for wholesale gasoline are observable and in 2009, refiner rack sales accounted for 60% of the total gasoline supplied in the US. See http://tonto.eia.doe.gov/dnav/pet/pet_cons_refmg_c_nus_epm0_mgalpd_a.htm and http://tonto.eia.doe.gov/dnav/pet/pet_cons_psup_dc_nus_mbbl_m.htm. The rest is sold to lessee-dealer stations at (unobserved) dealer-tank-wagon (DTW) prices and via transfer prices to refiner-operated stations.

[3] See The Federal Trade Commission, "Gasoline Price Changes: The Dynamics of Supply, Demand and Competition," 2005.

dynamics present in the gasoline industry which are difficult to explain with competitive or oligopolistic economic models.

The literature on rockets and feathers dates back to at least 1991 when Robert Bacon found evidence of an asymmetric response in gasoline prices in the UK. Since that time, others have found evidence of the phenomenon including Borenstein, Cameron, and Gilbert (1997, hereafter BCG), Lewis (forthcoming), Ye et. al. (2005), and most recently, Deltas (2008). These studies all utilize some form of an error correction model (outlined below) and consider some combination of crude oil prices, wholesale prices (rack or spot), and retail gasoline prices. They also vary by the geography they consider and how the data are aggregated over time (i.e., daily, weekly, or monthly). There are also several papers that, due to either a different data source or model, find no evidence of an asymmetric price response including Bachmeier and Griffin (2003) and Godby (2000). The former paper also tests BCG results using daily data; however they only focus on the transmission of crude oil to spot gasoline prices.

This paper is similar to BCG in that I analyze several different prices (crude oil, spot gasoline, rack, and retail prices) over a long period of time. However, unlike BCG who use weekly and bi-weekly data from the Lundberg Survey, I have access to daily data on all prices. I also avoid a modeling assumption by BCG (discussed below) which was questioned by Bachmeier and Griffin (2003) and instead use a more standard approach.

If it exists, there is little consensus on what causes the asymmetric response, though explanations range from consumer search costs, to explicit or implicit collusion, to inventory management by consumers. Deltas, for example, looks at how the asymmetric response varies with the level of retail market power and finds more asymmetry in markets with relatively more retail market power.[4] Lewis (forthcoming) and others posit

---

[4]Market power is proxied by the average markup observed in the market over his sample period. It is tempting to assume that markets in which firms face less competition will feature firms quickly passing on cost increases to consumers, and only slowly (or possibly never) passing on cost savings. Markets with many competing firms should feature perfect pass-through. For industry-wide cost changes, this is generally true, however the opposite results when the cost change is firm-specific. Bulow and Pfleiderer (1983) show that firm-specific cost changes are more completely passed through the less competitive is

that consumer search behavior could be causing the asymmetric response. If consumers are more likely to search for a low price when prices are expected to rise, then competition will be fierce when costs are rising and margins tight. However, if prices are falling, consumers may search less and this provides retailers with short-term market power and allows them to slowly lower prices and increase their margins. If this is the case, it still does not explain why asymmetric adjustment varies across time or across different geographic areas.

Asymmetric adjustment of downstream prices to changes in an upstream cost (such as a wholesale price) is generally divided into two forms: *amount asymmetry* and *pattern asymmetry*. Amount asymmetry occurs when the aggregate change over a period of time is different when costs are rising versus when they are falling. This asymmetry is not the focus of most studies because it would imply that the upstream and downstream prices would diverge over time, which is not the case with gasoline prices. Pattern asymmetry involves differences in the relative speed of pass-through. As an example, one may find evidence of pattern asymmetry if a 10% increase in wholesale prices leads to a 10% increase in retail prices after one week, but an equivalent decrease in wholesale prices leads to only a 5% decline in retail prices after one week. Consistent with the literature, I will focus my analysis on pattern asymmetry.

In this study, I look for pattern asymmetry in pass-through, and I vary the geography, the time aggregation, and products considered. I find the strongest evidence of pattern asymmetry in the rack to retail prices at both the city and national level. On average, retail prices rise more than four times as fast as they fall. Branded gasoline features significantly more asymmetry compared with unbranded gasoline.

Asymmetry varies significantly from year to year and across cities. For example, while in Los Angeles, the asymmetry of branded rack to retail price changes is fairly

---

the market. (See also, Ten Kate and Niels (2005).) The reason is that when faced with a cost decrease, say, firms with a greater market share will benefit relatively more from the increase in quantity demanded which more than offsets the lower revenue from passing on the cost decrease in the form of lower prices.

constant over time, in Phoenix, it is over four times as high in 2005 versus in 2007. Using weekly instead of daily data, tends to attenuate the evidence of asymmetry in some cases, though increases it in others.

The paper proceeds as follows. In section 2, I outline the model that I employ and specification tests that need to be run to justify its use. I discuss the data and provide basic descriptive statistics in section 3 and present the results of my model in section 4, including asymmetric pass-through results for different geographic areas, at different levels of time aggregation, and for different products. In section 5, I conclude and provide a brief outline of a complementary paper which seeks to explain why pass-through rates and asymmetry vary by city and over time.

2 Model

I estimate an error correction model (ECM) frequently used in the literature, though in various forms (e.g., Bachmeier and Griffin (2003)). I estimate two versions of the model: one which is run individually for each city (metro area)[5] and the other is a national-level model with fixed effects included for each city, which allows for different markups in each city.[6] The latter regression measures the average pass-through rate across all cities, while allowing the long-term relationship to vary by city. I allow for a difference in the pass-through of positive and negative upstream price changes.

While I estimate the model for several pairs of upstream and downstream prices, for simplicity, the following is the *rack to retail* pass-through model for a given city:

---

[5]Most of the metro areas in my sample are major cities. Some cities near state borders are split across state lines, so for example, Louisville, KY and Louisville, IN are separate metro areas. See figure A.1 for an example. This is important because often different types of gasoline (e.g., conventional, RFG, and California Air Resources Board (CARB) gasoline) are sold in different states.

[6]I use the term "national-level," though prices are not aggregated, but instead the specification includes prices from all major cities in my dataset.

$$\Delta Retail_t = \sum_{i=0}^{L_1^+} \beta_{1i}^+ \Delta^+ Rack_{t-i} + \sum_{i=0}^{L_1^-} \beta_{1i}^- \Delta^- Rack_{t-i} \tag{1}$$

$$+ \sum_{i=1}^{L_2^+} \beta_{2i}^+ \Delta^+ Retail_{t-i} + \sum_{i=1}^{L_2^-} \beta_{2i}^- \Delta^- Retail_{t-i}$$

$$+ \beta_3^+ \underbrace{\left(Retail_{t-1} - \gamma_0 - \gamma_1 Rack_{t-1}\right)}_{z_{t-1}^+}$$

$$+ \beta_3^- \underbrace{\left(Retail_{t-1} - \gamma_0 - \gamma_1 Rack_{t-1}\right)}_{z_{t-1}^-} + \epsilon_t.$$

Note $\Delta Retail_{t-i} = Retail_{t-i} - Retail_{t-(i-1)}$. Lag lengths are determined by minimizing the Bayesian Information Criterion (BIC):

$$BIC = K * log(N) + N * [Log(RSS/N)], \tag{2}$$

where K is the number of parameters to be estimated, N is the number of observations, and $RSS = \hat{\epsilon}'\hat{\epsilon}$ from equation 1. I could allow the lag lengths to vary separately for positive and negative changes as well as for rack and retail prices. However, since determining the optimal lag lengths for each price series, versus using a fixed (and equal) lag length for all, does not affect the qualitative results, in the analysis below I fix the lag length at 21 days in all regressions. This also allows me to compare regressions across cities and over time since I will utilize the same specification in each.

The expression $z_{t-1} = Retail_{t-1} - \gamma_0 - \gamma_1 Rack_{t-1}$ is the *error correction term*, and it captures the long-run relationship between the upstream and downstream prices. β_3^+ and β_3^- should both be negative: if retail prices are above their equilibrium level ($z_{t-1} > 0$), retail prices should fall and if they are below the level predicted by the rack price ($z_{t-1} < 0$), retail prices should rise.

Following the two-step method proposed by Engle and Granger (1987), I estimate γ_0

7

and γ_1 by running OLS on the following equation:

$$Retail_{t-1} = \gamma_0 + \gamma_1 Rack_{t-1} + z_{t-1}. \tag{3}$$

The residuals, z_{t-1}, are then inserted directly into the model.[7] BGC estimate the long-term relationship in the same step as the rest of the parameters and instrument for the upstream prices to control for possible endogeneity. As outlined in Bachmeier and Griffin (2003), this may lead to problems with the resulting estimates.[8] Once I obtain the residuals, I can estimate equation 1 by OLS.

The national-level regression is similar, though it includes city-level fixed effects in the error correction term:

$$Retail_{t-1} = \gamma_0 + \gamma_1 Rack_{t-1} + \sum_{i=2}^{27} \phi_i City_i + z_{t-1}. \tag{4}$$

As mentioned in the introduction, there are two potential types of asymmetry: amount and pattern. In terms of the model parameters, amount asymmetry would be of the form:

$$\sum_{i=0}^{L_1^+} \beta_{1i}^+ \neq \sum_{i=0}^{L_1^-} \beta_{1i}^-, \tag{5}$$

however, this cannot exist over the long-term since upstream and downstream prices do not tend to drift apart. Pattern asymmetry could be found if any one of the following

---

[7]Since the two series are cointegrated, the OLS regression yields super-consistent estimates of the γ parameters. The estimates can then be inserted into the model as if they were known parameters.

[8]BCG run a two-stage least squares regression and instrument for the upstream price with the crude oil price in England and a forward prices of crude in the US. However, while they reject the null that there is no endogeneity in the prices, their 2SLS and OLS estimates are very similar.

three conditions are met:

$$\beta_{1i}^+ \neq \beta_{1i}^- \text{ for some } i \tag{6}$$

$$|\beta_3^+| \neq |\beta_3^-| \tag{7}$$

$$L_1^+ \neq L_1^- \text{ or } L_2^+ \neq L_2^-. \tag{8}$$

The asymmetry in equation 6 is the one commonly analyzed in the literature. While the aggregate pass-through should be the same for positive and negative rack price changes, the pattern of the pass-through may be different. If any of the coefficients on the same lag are different, this is evidence of pattern asymmetry. The coefficients on the first lag, $\beta_{1,1}^+$ and $\beta_{1,1}^-$ are particularly important because they measure the contemporaneous speed of pass-through, assuming the model could be approximated as a first-order difference equation.

The second pattern asymmetry (noting again that β_3 should be negative reflecting mean-reversion) involves the speed at which relative prices return to their long-term equilibrium levels. We have evidence of the rockets and feathers type of asymmetry if this mean reversion is slower (closer to zero) when retail prices are above their long-term levels and faster (closer to one) when retail prices should be adjusting upwards toward their long-term levels.

Finally, if I allowed the BIC-optimum lag lengths to vary for positive and negative changes, further evidence of pattern asymmetry is obtained if the optimal lag lengths are different. Though this is often the case, I fix the lag lengths and focus most of my attention on asymmetries in contemporaneous pass-through and mean reversion via the error correction term.

3 Data and Descriptive Statistics

I combine two datasets to perform the analysis. Spot prices are available from Reuters via the Energy Information Administration (EIA) and rack and retail price data are from the Oil Price Information Service (OPIS). All data are available daily (I will discuss weekends and missing values below) from January 1999 through December 2009. Summary statistics are provided in tables 1, 2, and 3. All prices are reported in cents per gallon (cpg).

Spot prices include the price of West Texas Intermediate (WTI) crude oil at Cushing, Oklahoma. I also obtain the conventional regular and reformulated regular gasoline prices along with the RBOB[9] spot for New York harbor, the Gulf Coast, and Los Angeles. Spot prices are reported as of the close of day, Monday through Friday.

Spot Price	N	Min	Mean	Max	Std Dev	Date Range	Average Margin Over WTI
Conventional - NY	2,726	29.03	131.33	341.55	66.86	Jan 1999 - Dec 2009	16.93
Conventional - Gulf	2,726	27.00	130.69	487.25	68.43	Jan 1999 - Dec 2009	16.29
Conventional - LA	2,726	38.00	143.91	382.51	69.69	Jan 1999 - Dec 2009	29.51
RFG - NY	1,859	30.43	101.61	282.95	41.19	Jan 1999 - June 2006	18.24
RFG - Gulf	1,834	28.65	99.87	344.50	41.52	Jan 1999 - May 2006	17.66
RFG - LA	1,222	40.00	91.04	167.00	22.09	Jan 1999 - Nov 2003	28.04
RBOB - NY	1,340	75.33	188.64	357.60	56.37	July 2004 - Dec 2009	23.90
RBOB - Gulf	889	82.30	207.06	487.25	63.87	May 2006 - Dec 2009	26.09
RBOB - LA	1,679	78.00	188.54	389.60	62.30	Mar 2003 - Dec 2009	41.21
WTI	2,726	27.10	114.41	345.98	62.71	Jan 1999 - Dec 2009	-

Table 1: Daily Spot Prices (Cents per Gallon)

I use rack prices from OPIS for 20 U.S. cities. These rack prices are for the type of gasoline used in each city since many cities utilize different types of gasoline (conventional, RFG, etc.). In some cases, rack prices for different types of gasoline are reported in the same city. In these cases, I use the rack price that corresponds to the type of gasoline that is used in each retail market area. For example, the Fairfax, VA rack reports both conventional and RFG prices. Since I observe retail data for stations in

---

[9]Reformulated Blendstock for Oxygenate Blending.

Washington, DC, as well as the Virginia, Maryland, and West Virginia suburbs of DC, I match the RFG rack price to DC, VA, and MD since each uses primarily RFG, while the WV retail prices are matched to the conventional rack since that area primarily uses conventional gasoline. Rack prices are reported as of 9AM, Monday through Saturday, and are available for both branded and unbranded products.

	Border States	N	Min	Mean	Max	Std Dev	Date Range	Average Margin Over WTI
Atlanta (Conventional)		4,014	33.09	126.90	354.29	72.11	Jan 1997 - Dec 2009	25.17
Boston (RFG)		4,065	36.05	131.09	362.22	70.51	Jan 1997 - Dec 2009	29.05
Chicago (RFG)		4,066	38.94	135.05	363.34	70.77	Jan 1997 - Dec 2009	33.21
Cleveland (Conventional)		4,066	32.33	128.70	359.30	70.68	Jan 1997 - Dec 2009	26.97
Dallas (RFG)		4,066	34.65	129.35	356.63	71.14	Jan 1997 - Dec 2009	27.73
Denver (Conventional)		4,066	33.37	129.55	364.76	70.82	Jan 1997 - Dec 2009	27.64
Detroit (Conventional)		4,066	31.10	128.73	361.20	71.17	Jan 1997 - Dec 2009	27.04
Fairfax (Conventional)	WV	4,066	34.46	125.95	351.70	70.12	Jan 1997 - Dec 2009	23.76
Fairfax (RFG)	DC, MD, VA	4,066	37.11	130.35	356.28	71.52	Jan 1997 - Dec 2009	28.49
Houston (RFG)		4,065	33.77	127.19	355.03	70.71	Jan 1997 - Dec 2009	25.37
Los Angeles (CARB)		2,825	59.28	174.35	392.91	66.58	Dec 2000 - Dec 2009	47.56
Louisville (Conventional)	IN	4,049	32.66	128.32	355.70	70.66	Jan 1997 - Dec 2009	26.29
Louisville (RFG)	KY	2,857	39.65	160.73	376.64	77.56	Feb 1998 - Dec 2009	40.54
Miami (Conventional)		4,066	34.84	126.63	353.51	70.97	Jan 1997 - Dec 2009	24.64
Minneapolis (Conventional)		4,064	35.18	130.67	357.47	70.81	Jan 1997 - Dec 2009	28.90
New Orleans (Conventional)		4,066	32.81	124.01	350.88	69.96	Jan 1997 - Dec 2009	21.86
Newark (RFG)		3,803	38.82	134.25	355.16	69.20	Mar 1997 - Dec 2009	27.17
Phoenix (Conventional)		4,066	43.60	140.32	366.58	71.25	Jan 1997 - Dec 2009	39.44
Salt Lake City (Conventional)		4,065	37.05	134.35	367.52	69.56	Jan 1997 - Dec 2009	32.22
San Francisco (CARB)		2,809	59.23	171.41	375.37	65.27	Jan 2001 - Dec 2009	44.24
Seattle (Conventional)		4,066	41.66	135.62	364.57	70.37	Jan 1997 - Dec 2009	34.19
St Louis (Conventional)	IL	4,065	31.94	128.38	355.41	71.62	Jan 1997 - Dec 2009	26.62
St Louis (RFG)	MO	3,337	57.92	149.81	359.20	66.52	May 1999 - Dec 2009	32.47

Racks that service multiple states with different types of wholesale gasoline are indicated in the "Boarder States" column. For example, the Fairfax, VA rack sells RFG to stations in Washington DC and its nearby suburbs, while it sells conventional gasoline to stations in West Virginia.

Table 2: Daily Rack Prices (Cents per Gallon)

Finally, I utilize pre-tax retail price data from OPIS for the 27 retail metro areas all within the 20 cities for which I have rack prices. Retail prices are (usually) end of the day prices as they are recorded from the last swipe of a consumer's "fleet-card" on a given day.[10] OPIS averages all the prices they receive each day (at most one from each station) to determine the price for the metro area. After 2001, the prices are reported every day of the week. OPIS samples over 100,000 stations each day and covers branded and unbranded stations. The three most expensive cities for retail gasoline in 2008 were

---

[10]See http://www.opisretail.com/methodology.html for more information on OPIS's retail data. More than one-half of the stations in the OPIS sample report a price each day, though the sample of stations may change from day to day.

Miami, San Francisco, and Washington DC. These three cities also featured the highest retail markups over the wholesale price.

	N	Min	Mean	Max	Std Dev	Date Range	Average Margin Over Rack
Atlanta	3,817	49.35	152.19	346.67	69.64	Jan 1999 - Dec 2009	9.35
Boston	3,817	58.16	163.20	366.50	68.77	Jan 1999 - Dec 2009	16.58
Chicago	3,817	55.82	163.88	365.56	70.41	Jan 1999 - Dec 2009	13.25
Cleveland	3,817	45.37	156.72	358.05	68.93	Jan 1999 - Dec 2009	12.30
Dallas	3,817	50.31	156.40	359.55	70.41	Jan 1999 - Dec 2009	11.14
Denver	3,816	49.03	158.37	360.39	70.36	Jan 1999 - Dec 2009	13.39
Detroit	3,817	46.10	155.22	360.01	69.34	Jan 1999 - Dec 2009	10.71
Houston	3,817	51.19	154.57	357.81	70.11	Jan 1999 - Dec 2009	11.64
Los Angeles	3,816	56.39	175.32	392.76	71.13	Jan 1999 - Dec 2009	13.46
Louisville IN	3,815	42.28	153.94	364.86	69.26	Jan 1999 - Dec 2009	10.20
Louisville KY	3,816	47.53	163.66	389.74	72.31	Jan 1999 - Dec 2009	7.51
Miami	3,817	68.21	177.18	383.47	73.14	Jan 1999 - Dec 2009	34.61
Minneapolis MN	3,817	54.06	158.88	360.77	68.43	Jan 1999 - Dec 2009	12.58
Minneapolis WI	3,815	51.50	158.18	353.03	68.37	Jan 1999 - Dec 2009	11.78
New Orleans	3,815	56.13	157.52	362.36	70.84	Jan 1999 - Dec 2009	18.00
Newark	3,816	57.82	163.97	367.73	69.48	Jan 1999 - Dec 2009	19.41
New York City	3,817	60.55	166.93	365.48	68.54	Jan 1999 - Dec 2009	22.32
Pheonix	3,816	54.55	167.61	376.72	69.38	Jan 1999 - Dec 2009	10.50
Salt Lake City	3,816	46.67	158.08	373.46	70.96	Jan 1999 - Dec 2009	8.48
San Francisco	3,815	80.72	188.67	390.37	67.09	Jan 1999 - Dec 2009	28.24
Seattle	3,816	63.10	171.78	384.57	69.82	Jan 1999 - Dec 2009	20.03
St Louis IL	3,817	43.00	150.40	351.03	68.03	Jan 1999 - Dec 2009	6.27
St Louis MO	3,816	42.16	155.76	362.64	70.02	Jan 1999 - Dec 2009	6.56
Washington DC	3,756	58.14	174.30	380.73	73.39	Jan 1999 - Dec 2009	26.97
Washington MD	3,817	54.27	165.07	368.13	71.50	Jan 1999 - Dec 2009	18.97
Washington VA	3,817	50.87	160.03	363.64	70.84	Jan 1999 - Dec 2009	13.97
Washington WV	3,815	43.27	156.50	360.02	71.32	Jan 1999 - Dec 2009	14.95

This table shows statistics by "retail market area" as reported by OPIS. Prices are generated using Fleet Card purchases from all stations in the area.

Table 3: Daily Retail Prices (Cents per Gallon)

Given the different reporting times of day for each price series, when running regressions using daily data, it is important that lags are used where appropriate. For example, when considering the speed of pass-through from rack to retail, I can consider the effect for the same time stamp since end of day retail prices have a chance to adjust to a change in the rack price observed at the beginning of the day. However, in the spot to rack pass-through regressions, I use the lagged spot price because these two price series are reported at the same time of day.

	Border	Branded		Unbranded		Proportion
	States	N	Mean	N	Mean	Unbranded > Branded
Atlanta (Conventional)		4,014	126.90	4,002	123.81	0.049
Boston (RFG)		4,065	131.09	4,066	126.20	0.039
Chicago (RFG)		4,066	135.05	4,066	131.75	0.042
Cleveland (Conventional)		4,066	128.70	4,062	125.90	0.072
Dallas (RFG)		4,066	129.35	4,066	126.67	0.083
Denver (Conventional)		4,066	129.55	4,066	127.07	0.066
Detroit (Conventional)		4,066	128.73	4,016	125.44	0.069
Fairfax (Conventional)	WV	4,066	125.95	4,004	123.60	0.065
Fairfax (RFG)	DC, MD, VA	4,066	130.35	4,066	126.69	0.050
Houston (RFG)		4,065	127.19	4,065	124.38	0.071
Los Angeles (CARB)		2,825	174.35	2,582	176.58	0.282
Louisville (Conventional)	IN	4,049	128.32	4,062	124.78	0.051
Louisville (RFG)	KY	2,857	160.73	3,723	144.23	0.128
Miami (Conventional)		4,066	126.63	4,066	123.64	0.041
Minneapolis (Conventional)		4,064	130.67	4,066	127.65	0.039
New Orleans (Conventional)		4,066	124.01	4,066	120.77	0.035
Newark (RFG)		3,803	134.25	3,809	129.57	0.052
Phoenix (Conventional)		4,066	140.32	4,066	134.14	0.142
Salt Lake City (Conventional)		4,065	134.35	4,065	131.96	0.090
San Francisco (CARB)		2,809	171.41	2,412	178.16	0.287
Seattle (Conventional)		4,066	135.62	4,066	130.89	0.164
St Louis (Conventional)	IL	4,065	128.38	4,025	124.99	0.066
St Louis (RFG)	MO	3,337	149.81	3,323	150.13	0.270

Table 4: Branded versus Unbranded Rack Prices (Cents per Gallon)

In table 4, I report statistics on branded versus unbranded rack prices. Generally, unbranded gasoline is more homogeneous across refiners because it includes only a generic package of additives and lacks a brand name premium. Therefore, in most cases, branded gasoline is about 5 cents more expensive than unbranded. However, as evidence in the right-hand column shows, at times the unbranded price actually exceeds the branded price and this happens quite often in Los Angeles, San Francisco, and St. Louis. Many of these *inversions* follow supply shocks (e.g., hurricanes and refinery outages) as refiners may be giving priority to their branded customers to maintain the brand image, resulting in a more severe supply reduction for unbranded gasoline. Whatever the cause, below I investigate the asymmetric response for branded and unbranded fuel separately.

3.1 Data Issues

Before focusing on the results, there are a few issues with the data that need to be addressed. I run my regressions at both a daily and a weekly frequency. Weekly data was generated as the simple average of the daily series. This means that sometimes the average is over five days, other times six days, four days, etc. Early in the sample, the data suffer from many missing values, though starting in 2002, the data are much more complete. Therefore, I restrict the regressions to dates from January 2002 - December 2009.

Due to holidays, etc, there are still some missing values in the daily data. Instead of interpolating on each of these days, I do the following:

1. Include any day that has data on both the upstream and downstream price.

2. Do not include any date that is missing both the upstream and downstream price.

3. Include a partial observation if it occurs on Monday - Friday, leaving the missing value in the data.[11]

This means that the duration between observations is usually one day (adjacent days) or three days (for weekends) though at times may be longer if both prices are missing for a period of time. I have analyzed the distribution of changes in all the prices as it varies by the number of days between adjacent non-missing observations. I find that there is almost no "weekend effect" in that the changes in price from Friday to Monday have the same distribution as the changes on adjacent days. However, there are a few longer periods in the data with missing values and the distribution of changes is much wider. Therefore, I control for these large jumps by including a dummy variable which equals one if any of the changes on the upstream or downstream price are for a period of five

---

[11]The reason I include the partial observation instead of dropping it is to eliminate situations where two lagged differences are included in an observation, one over adjacent days, and the other over a much longer number of days. In effect, this method results in dropping several observations when I estimate the model, but reduces the number of long gaps between consequative observations.

days or more. With this set of observations, lags are formed and if missing values are present in any observation, it is removed from the analysis.[12]

Finally, at one time the spot price for RFG was for reformulated gasoline blended with MTBE, which has now been banned in most states.[13] It has been replaced by the RBOB spot price, which is RFG that will eventually get blended with an oxygenate (typically ethanol). In New York and LA, there is some overlap in the two series so I create my complete spot price for RFG as the old RFG spot for the early part of the sample, and as soon as the RBOB spot is available, I switch to that price. The two prices are similar to each other during the overlap period.[14] For the Gulf Coast, there is no overlap (the RFG spot ends on one day and the RBOB spot begins being reported on the very next day) so I concatenate the two series to form my complete RFG spot price. However, the RBOB price on its first day being reported is 38 cents higher than the RFG spot on the previous day.[15] I have done robustness checks by only running the regression using dates where I observe the RFG spot price and the results are very similar.

4 Results

Before analyzing the results, it is important to test for stationarity of the regressors. I run Augmented Dickey Fuller (ADF) tests which show that all price series do indeed have a unit root so first differencing is necessary. I then run another ADF test on each set of price series together and confirm that the upstream and downstream price series are cointegrated (i.e., the residuals from the long-run regression equations 3 and 4 are

---

[12]Removing observations only *after* lags are formed guarantees that the lagged differences in a given observation are all over approximately the same (small) duration of time.

[13]In others, the liability protection has been removed so refiners are reluctant to use it.

[14]A simple regression of the RFG spot on the RBOB spot during the overlap yields a slope coefficient of 0.94 for NY and 0.95 for LA.

[15]Compared with mean absolute day to day changes for RFG and RBOB of 2.6 and 5.1 cents respectively.

stationary).[16] Therefore, estimating the long-term relationship in the first stage provides super-consistent estimates which can be entered into the model directly. Durbin Watson tests for autocorrelation correlation are also run and fail to reject the hypothesis that there is no autocorrelation in the residuals for each model.

I divide the results into several sections which consider the differences in pattern asymmetry among different price relationships, across cities and in the national regression, by the time aggregation of the data, for branded versus unbranded wholesale gasoline, and over time. Finally, I show formal F-tests of pattern asymmetry for each type of model.

4.1 Price Relationships

I investigate pass-through asymmetry for combinations of the crude oil price, the gasoline spot price, the branded and unbranded rack prices, and the retail price series. The following tables and figures summarize the results of equation 4, which incorporate data from all cities and includes city-level fixed effects in the long-term first-stage regression. The relationships include the following:

1. Crude oil price to the gasoline spot price, the rack prices, and the retail price.[17]

2. Closest gasoline spot price to the rack prices and the retail price.[18]

3. Rack prices to the retail price.

Complete results for one of these regressions (rack to retail) is shown in table A.1 in the appendix. However, following the literature on asymmetric pass-through, it is much easier to present the results graphically. The reason is that a one-time change in the upstream price will have an immediate effect on the downstream price, but the

---

[16]ADF test statistics on the rack to retail price relationship are all greater than six compared with a 5% critical value of 3.33 from MacKinnon (2010).

[17]I estimate the crude to spot relationship for each of the six spot prices available on EIA's website: conventional gasoline and RFG in NY, Houston, and LA.

[18]I use the NY spot price for Boston and Newark. I use the LA spot price for LA, San Francisco, Phoenix, Salt Lake City and Seattle. For the rest, I use the Gulf Coast spot price.

total effect may be drawn out over a period of days and include both the short-term speed of adjustment (the β_1 terms in equation 1), the own-lag effects (the β_2 terms), and the long-term error correction effects (the β_3 terms). For this reason, I present impulse response functions which trace out the effects of a ten cent per gallon change (positive or negative) in the upstream price on the downstream price over a period of several days following the shock. The 95% confidence bands are also shown in each graph.[19]

Figures 1 and 2 below, along with figures A.2, A.3, A.4, and A.5 in the appendix display the impulse response function tracing out the effect on the downstream price of a 10 cpg change in the upstream price. While each of the figures shows some kind of asymmetric response, the rockets and feathers type (where the response time of positive shocks exceeds negative shocks) is strongest in the rack to retail and spot to retail relationships. However, while the asymmetry in both of these relationships becomes statistically insignificant after about seven to ten days, the asymmetry in spot to retail prices is significantly smaller than rack to retail. A weaker (and sometimes reverse) asymmetry is shown in the crude to gasoline spot, rack, and retail price regressions.

Bacon (1991) found a similar asymmetry in rack to retail prices, while Bachmeier and Griffin (2003) find no evidence of asymmetry in the crude oil to gasoline spot price transmission, consistent with my results. BCG (1997) do not find any significant asymmetry in the spot to retail relationship, though their study relies on bi-weekly data.

4.2 Individual City Results

The evidence of asymmetries found in the previous section is mostly confirmed by regressions run at the individual city level. In table 5, I present results on the difference in the first coefficients on the upstream price for positive and negative changes. Though a complete picture of pass-through asymmetry can only be seen from an impulse response

---

[19]To account for possible nonlinearities in the relationships between the upstream and downstream prices, I consider an upstream price increase from 200 cpg to 210 cpg and a corresponding decrease from 210 cpg to 200 cpg.

17

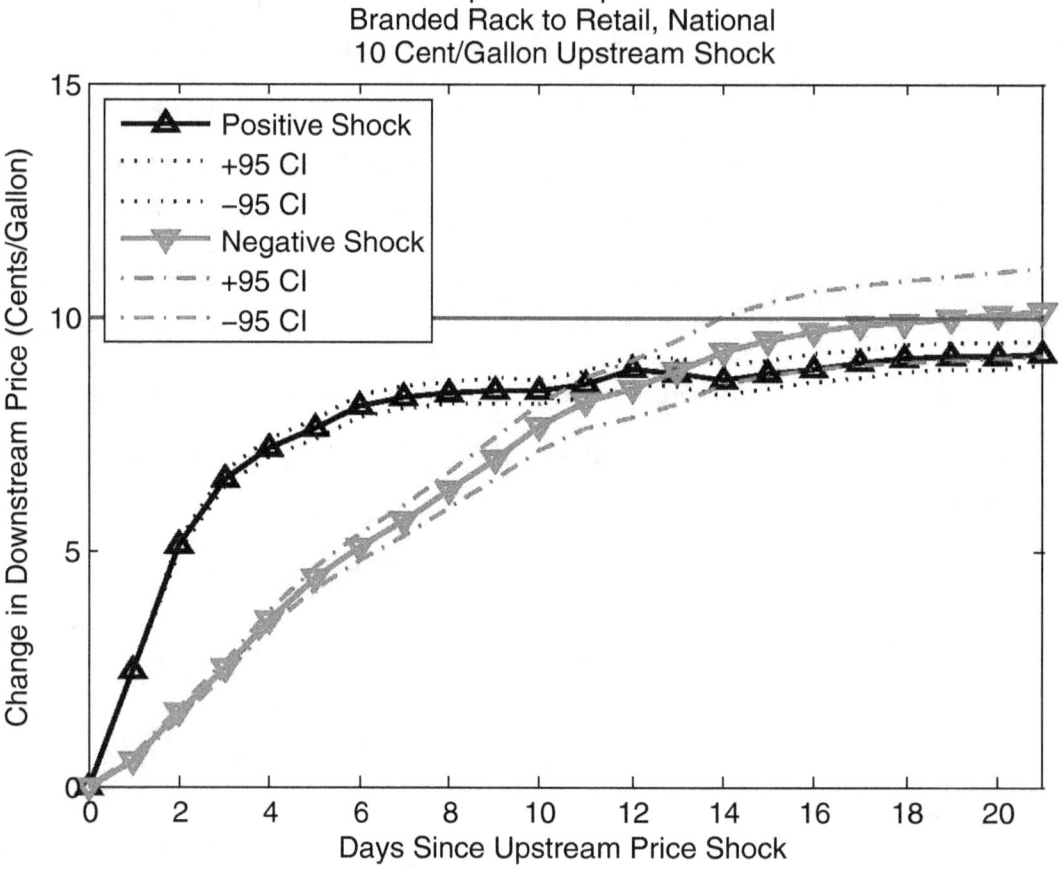

Figure 1: Impulse Response Function: Rack to Retail Prices, All Cities Included

graph, this first coefficient embodies the *speed of pass-through* if we think of the model as approximating a first-order difference equation.

I include the difference by city and for each of the city-specific price relationships. The difference in the β_1 coefficients in the crude oil to rack and retail price relationships are mostly insignificant or have a reverse asymmetry as measured by the speed coefficient. The spot to rack regressions reveal asymmetry in several cities, including Detroit, Miami, and St. Louis. The final two columns on rack to retail prices again confirm the strong asymmetry in all cities as was found in the previous section. The asymmetry is the strongest in Cleveland, Detroit, Louisville, and Minneapolis, while it is weakest in San Francisco and the West Virginia suburbs of Washington DC.

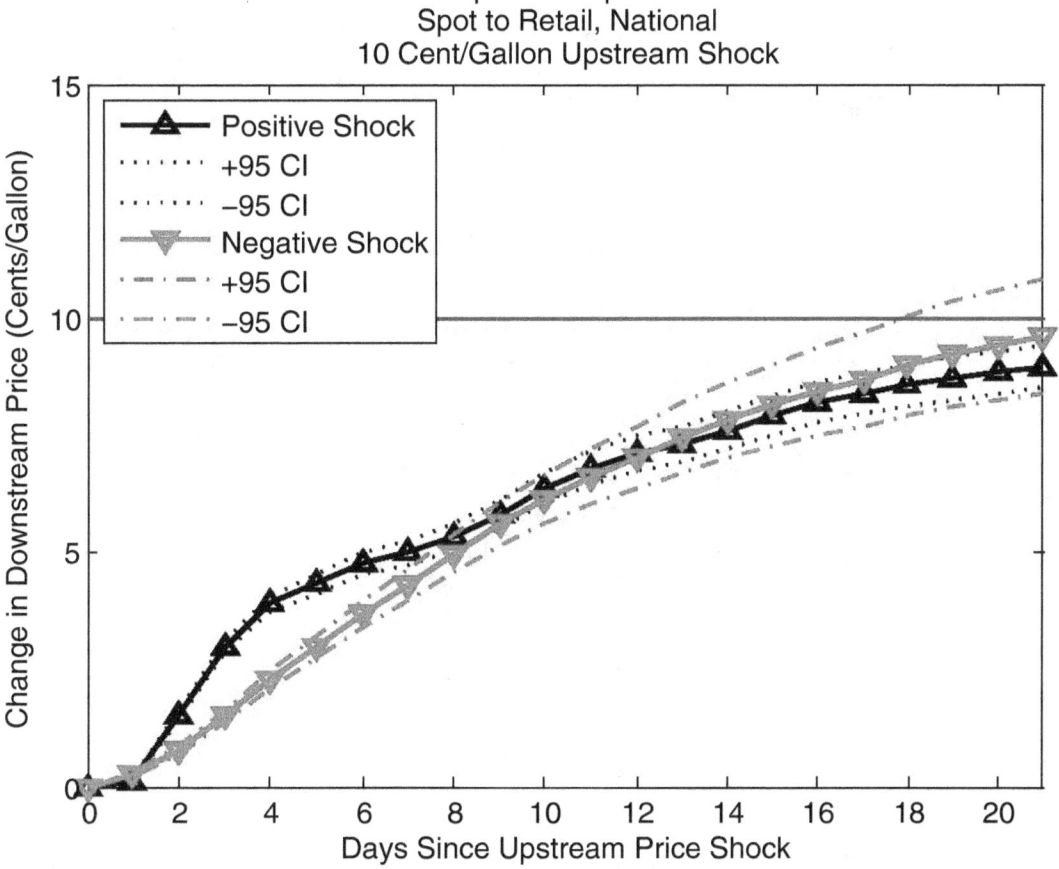

Figure 2: Impulse Response Function: Gasoline Spot to Retail Prices, All Cities Included

In table 6, I present the results on the form of asymmetry shown in equation 7: the difference between the positive and negative coefficients on the error correction term. The results for the rack to retail relationships are similar to above, and the long-term correction asymmetry appears more in the crude to rack and retail price relationships, while it has the opposite sign in spot to rack price regressions.

The type of fuel utilized in each city is also related to the degree of pass-through asymmetry. For example, St. Louis IL, Louisville IN, and Washington WV all utilize conventional gasoline and all have lower asymmetry than their neighboring retail metro areas which utilize RFG.

While the differences in the speed of adjustment and error correction terms provides

19

$$\beta_1^+ - \beta_1^-$$

	WTI to Branded Rack	WTI to Unbranded Rack	WTI to Retail	Spot to Branded Rack	Spot to Unbranded Rack	Branded Rack to Retail	Unbranded Rack to Retail
Atlanta	-0.20***	-0.09	-0.02	0.01	0.03	0.23***	0.14***
Boston	-0.10***	-0.12*	-0.05***	0.03	0.12***	0.14***	0.07***
Chicago	-0.04	-0.04	-0.06**	0.06**	-0.02	0.13***	0.09***
Cleveland	-0.09*	0.10	-0.21***	0.05*	-0.06	0.31***	0.21***
Dallas	-0.21***	-0.11*	-0.05***	0.03	0.02	0.12***	0.07***
Denver	-0.09**	-0.11**	-0.02	0.02	0.03	0.11***	0.08***
Detroit	-0.01	0.16**	-0.09**	0.08***	0.09**	0.32***	0.20***
Washington DC	-0.14***	-0.05	-0.08***	-0.01	-0.10***	0.15***	0.08***
Washington MD	-0.14***	-0.05	-0.03	-0.01	-0.10***	0.13***	0.06***
Washington VA	-0.14***	-0.05	-0.03*	-0.01	-0.10***	0.12***	0.08***
Washington WV	-0.14***	0.06	-0.10***	0.05***	-0.04	0.07***	0.01
Houston	-0.14***	-0.02	-0.06***	0.00	0.13***	0.14***	0.06***
Los Angeles	-0.03	-0.13	-0.01	0.02	0.07	0.16***	0.01**
Louisville IN	-0.20***	-0.10	-0.15***	0.00	-0.01	0.27***	0.16***
Louisville KY	-0.19***	-0.08	-0.19**	-0.04	-0.10***	0.37***	0.27***
Miami	-0.16***	-0.15**	-0.07***	0.04**	0.20***	0.15***	0.07***
Minneapolis St Paul MN	-0.08	-0.16**	-0.17***	0.07***	-0.17***	0.38***	0.31***
Minneapolis St Paul WI	-0.08	-0.16**	-0.13***	0.07***	-0.17***	0.08***	0.07***
New Orleans	-0.23***	-0.08	-0.04**	0.01	0.06**	0.13***	0.05***
Newark	-0.10***	-0.14**	-0.07***	0.02	-0.08***	0.19***	0.10***
New York	-0.10***	-0.14**	-0.06***	0.02	-0.08***	0.11***	0.05***
Phoenix	0.05*	-0.12*	-0.03*	0.02	0.01	0.11***	0.04***
Salt Lake City	0.02	-0.01	-0.01	0.02**	0.01	0.16***	0.11***
San Francisco	-0.02	-0.23***	0.02	0.04**	0.01	0.08***	0.00
Seattle	-0.04*	-0.16***	-0.02*	0.01	0.07**	0.15***	0.04***
St Louis IL	-0.03	0.04	-0.06	0.10***	0.13***	0.20***	0.15***
St Louis MO	0.04	0.21**	-0.10*	0.06**	0.17***	0.32***	0.16***

Difference in positive and negative speed coefficients. Positive and significant differences are evidence of rockets and feathers. ***, **, * significant at the 1%, 5% and 10% levels respectively.

Table 5: Asymmetry in Difference in First Coefficients on Lagged Upstream Price

a first approximation of the asymmetric adjustment, a better measure would account for the overall price path resulting from prices rocketing up following cost increases and feathering down following cost decreases. Therefore, I first calculate the impulse response function for negative and positive shocks and then calculate the retail price under two regimes:

1. Following a downward cost shock, retail prices feather down at the rate seen in the data.

2. Following a downward cost shock, retail prices rocket down at the same rate they rocket up following cost increases.

	WTI to Branded Rack	WTI to Unbranded Rack	WTI to Retail	Spot to Branded Rack	Spot to Unbranded Rack	Branded Rack to Retail	Unbranded Rack to Retail
				$\beta_3^+ - \beta_3^-$			
Atlanta	0.03***	0.05***	-0.01	-0.22***	-0.14***	-0.01	0.02**
Boston	0.01	0.01	0.00	-0.06***	-0.03	0.02***	0.01***
Chicago	0.00	0.02	0.01***	-0.09***	-0.04*	0.09***	0.08***
Cleveland	0.03**	0.06***	0.06***	-0.09***	-0.12***	0.32***	0.05***
Dallas	0.02*	0.05***	0.00	-0.26***	-0.22***	0.03***	0.04***
Denver	0.01	0.03**	0.00	-0.04***	-0.03	0.05***	0.04***
Detroit	0.02*	0.01	0.03***	-0.10***	-0.06***	0.11***	0.03
Washington DC	0.03***	0.06***	-0.01	-0.20***	-0.20***	0.00	0.01
Washington MD	0.03***	0.06***	0.00	-0.20***	-0.20***	0.01	0.01***
Washington VA	0.03***	0.06***	0.00	-0.20***	-0.20***	0.01*	0.01***
Washington WV	0.02*	0.03	0.01	-0.29***	-0.13***	0.04***	0.02*
Houston	0.02**	0.04**	0.00	-0.29***	-0.28***	0.02***	0.02***
Los Angeles	0.01**	0.00	0.00*	-0.01	0.06	0.00	0.01***
Louisville IN	0.02	0.05***	0.04***	-0.12***	-0.07**	0.14***	0.13***
Louisville KY	0.02*	0.03*	0.04**	-0.14***	-0.03	0.19***	0.20***
Miami	0.03***	0.05***	0.00	-0.38***	-0.31***	0.02***	0.02***
Minneapolis St Paul MN	0.03***	0.04**	0.04***	-0.04**	-0.05**	0.24***	0.23***
Minneapolis St Paul WI	0.03***	0.04**	0.01	-0.04**	-0.05**	0.04***	0.04***
New Orleans	0.03***	0.05***	0.01	-0.39***	-0.41***	0.03***	0.03***
Newark	0.01	0.03**	0.00	-0.08***	-0.08**	0.02***	0.01***
New York	0.01	0.03**	0.00	-0.08***	-0.08**	0.02***	0.01***
Phoenix	0.01*	0.04***	0.00	-0.02**	-0.17***	0.00	0.01***
Salt Lake City	0.00	0.01	0.00	-0.02***	-0.02***	0.02***	0.03***
San Francisco	0.02**	-0.01	0.01**	-0.03**	-0.01	0.00	0.01***
Seattle	0.00	0.00	0.00	-0.02***	-0.06***	0.00	0.01***
St Louis IL	0.02	0.04**	0.03**	-0.06***	0.04	0.06***	0.05***
St Louis MO	0.01	-0.03*	0.04***	-0.05**	-0.08***	0.14***	0.04**

Difference in positive and error correction coefficients. Positive and significant differences are evidence of rockets and feathers. ***, **, * significant at the 1%, 5% and 10% levels respectively.

Table 6: Asymmetry in the Difference in Coefficients on the Error Correction Term

Calculating the average price in each regime and computing the difference between the two yields the total cost to the consumer of the asymmetric adjustment. I do this analysis for each city and the resulting asymmetry is reported in figure 3.

Louisville, IN features the largest asymmetry with prices almost 5 cpg higher when they feather down instead of rocket down (even though its speed of adjustment estimate was lower than neighboring Louisville, KY). Other cities, such as, Newark, Cleveland, Salt Lake City, and Washington DC also show relatively more asymmetry, while Washington WV and Minneapolis WI (both conventional gasoline users) have the least asymmetry. The loss in the unbranded rack to retail asymmetry is smaller in all cities

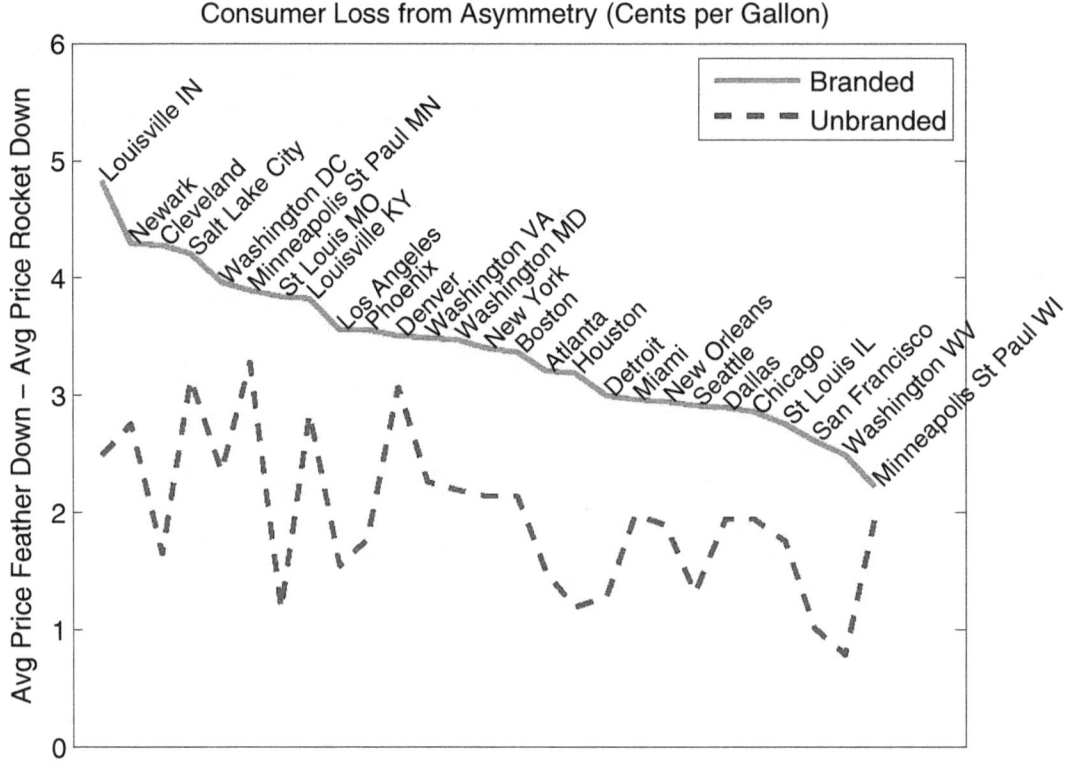

Figure 3: Consumer Loss from Asymmetric Adjustment

averaging around 2 cpg.

4.3   Time Aggregation

One of the major differences between the various studies in the extant literature is the frequency of the data used. Many rely on less frequent, bi-weekly or monthly data simply because it it more widely available. In this section, I consider the effect of using daily versus weekly data on the likelihood of finding evidence of pass-through asymmetry.

Figure 4 shows the same impulse response function for crude to rack prices, but the top panel uses daily data while the bottom panel uses average weekly prices. While, in general, both show a lack of asymmetry, the time required to reach complete pass-through is about a week in the daily regression and over two weeks in the weekly regression. Important day-to-day variation is being smoothed, which masks the pass-through dynamics

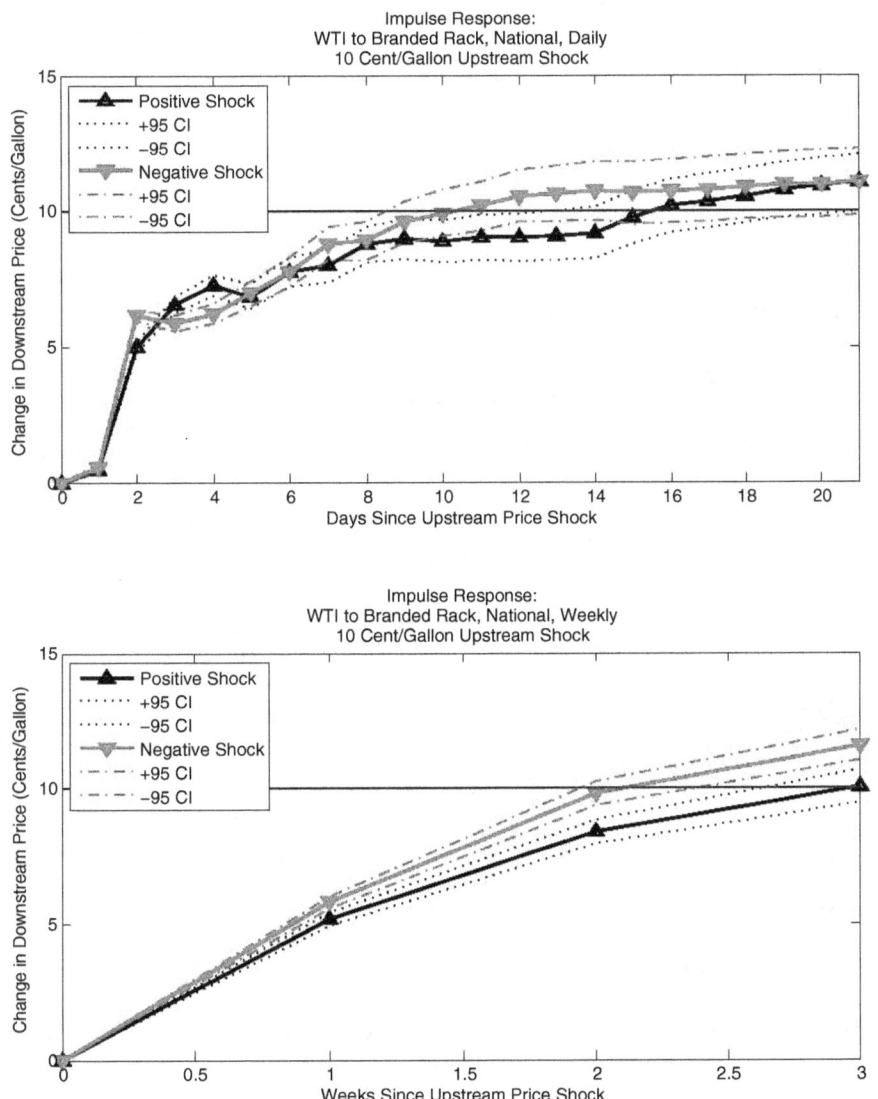

Figure 4: Frequency Analysis: Daily vs Weekly, Crude to Rack

between the two prices.

The results are similar when considering rack to retail prices in figure 5. Both impulse response functions show evidence of asymmetry though the pattern of the asymmetry is different. While the asymmetry disappears in ten days in the daily regression, it continues in the weekly regression for about three weeks when pass-through of the negative shock is finally completed.

4.4   Branded versus Unbranded

Branded wholesale gasoline is generally a few cents more expensive than unbranded gasoline given the former has proprietary additives (and a brand-name premium) included. However, at times, the unbranded price will exceed the branded price, and this occurs especially following negative supply shocks. As shown in figure 6, the (first lag) asymmetry for branded gasoline is significantly higher than for unbranded gasoline in almost every city.

Therefore, while the unbranded price may "rocket up" more quickly than the branded price following a supply shock, the speed at which it retreats back to equilibrium levels is slower for the branded price. In some cities, such as, Seattle and Los Angeles, the difference in asymmetry is very large with branded prices being more than twice as asymmetric compared with unbranded prices.[20] In future work, I will investigate these relationships further, specifically considering how the asymmetric response varies for day-to-day price movements compared with the dynamics following major supply disruptions.

---

[20]The result that unbranded gasoline prices exhibit less asymmetry may be consistent with the literature that claim heterogeneous consumer search costs are the cause of asymmetric adjustment. Consumers who buy branded gasoline are likely more loyal to a single brand, while unbranded buyers are more likely to shop around for the best price. A negative cost shock would be passed on more quickly to unbranded prices than to branded prices, reducing the asymmetry in the unbranded price relationship.

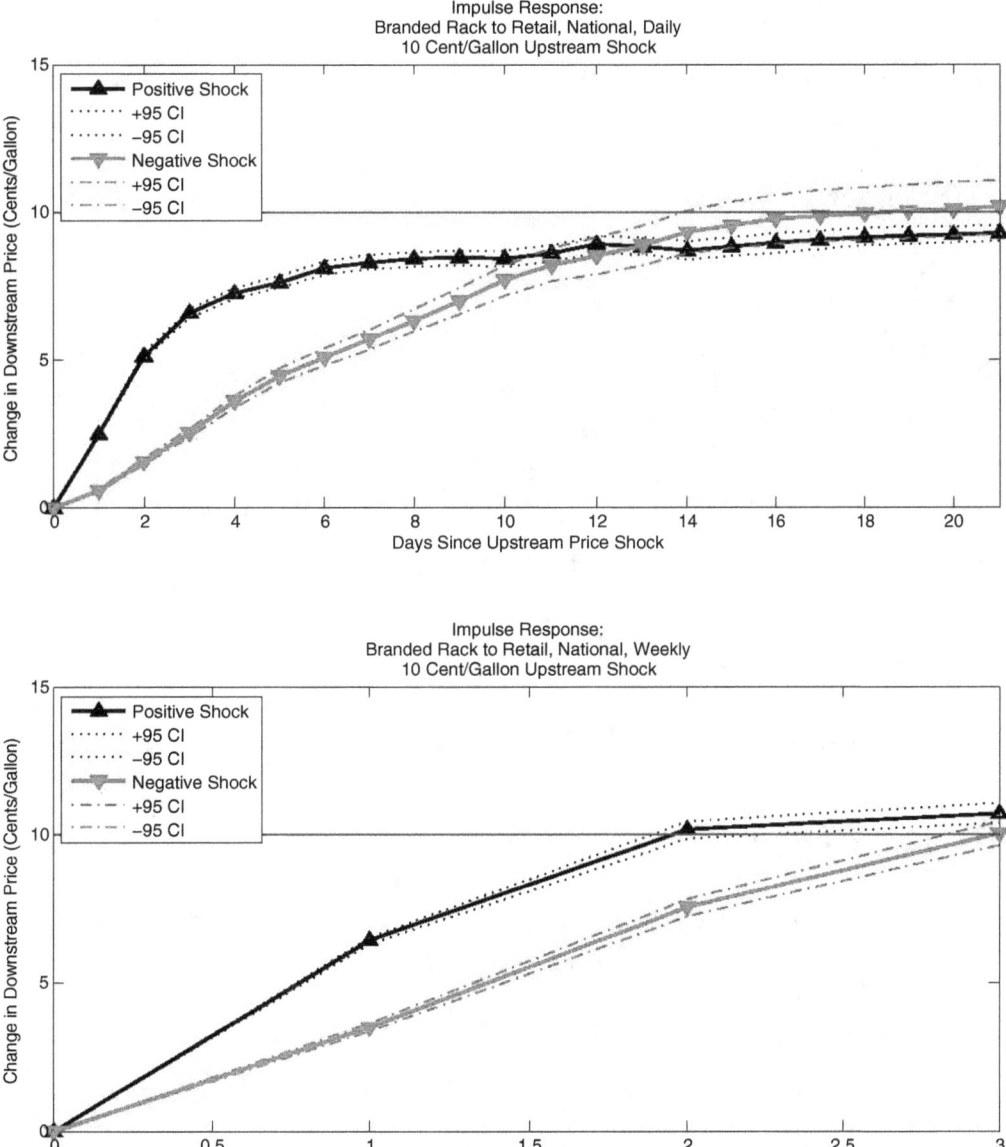

Figure 5: Frequency Analysis: Daily vs Weekly, Rack to Retail

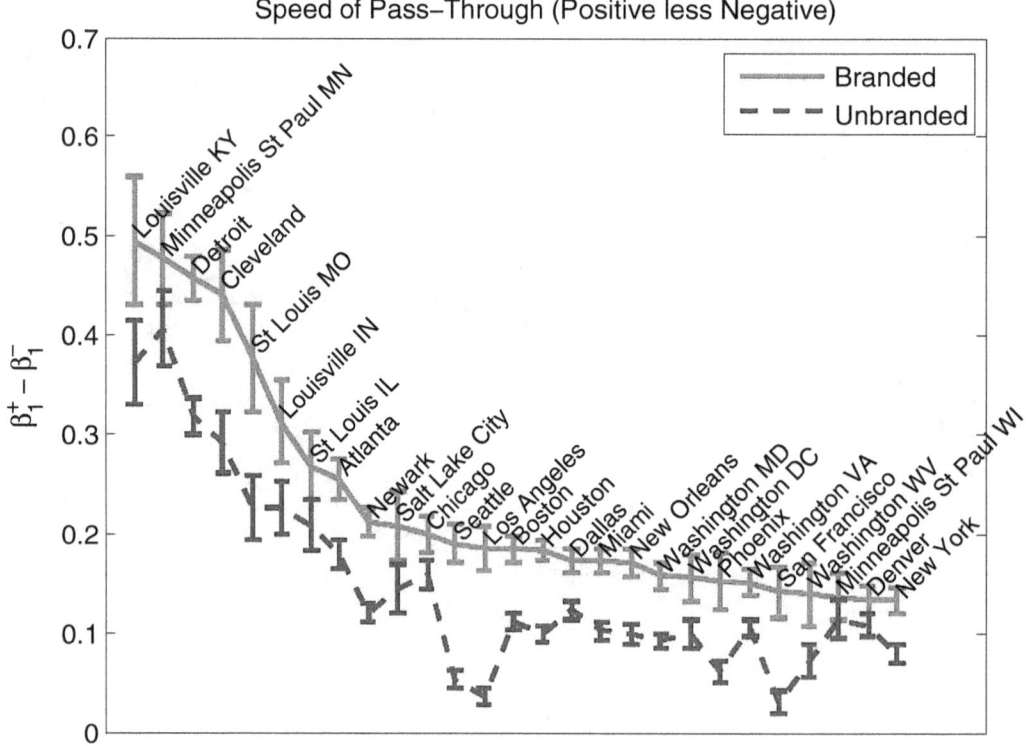

Figure 6: Branded vs Unbranded Analysis, Rack to Retail (95% confidence bands shown)

4.5 Differences Over Time

Finally, in figure 7 below and figure A.6 in the appendix, I investigate how pass-through asymmetry has changed over time. For this analysis, I estimate my model at a daily frequency for both branded and unbranded gasoline, but I run 80 separate overlapping regressions on a 12-month window of data centered on each month in the data. I then calculate the total loss due to asymmetry under the two regimes laid out above.

The asymmetry in pass-through from rack prices to retail prices varies significantly from year to year and peaks in 2005, possibly because 2005 was the most active hurricane season in history. In 2009, pass-through asymmetry cost consumers about 2 cpg on branded gasoline and between 1 and 1.5 cpg on unbranded gasoline. This assumes that consumers purchase their gas uniformly across all days no matter if prices are rising or falling.

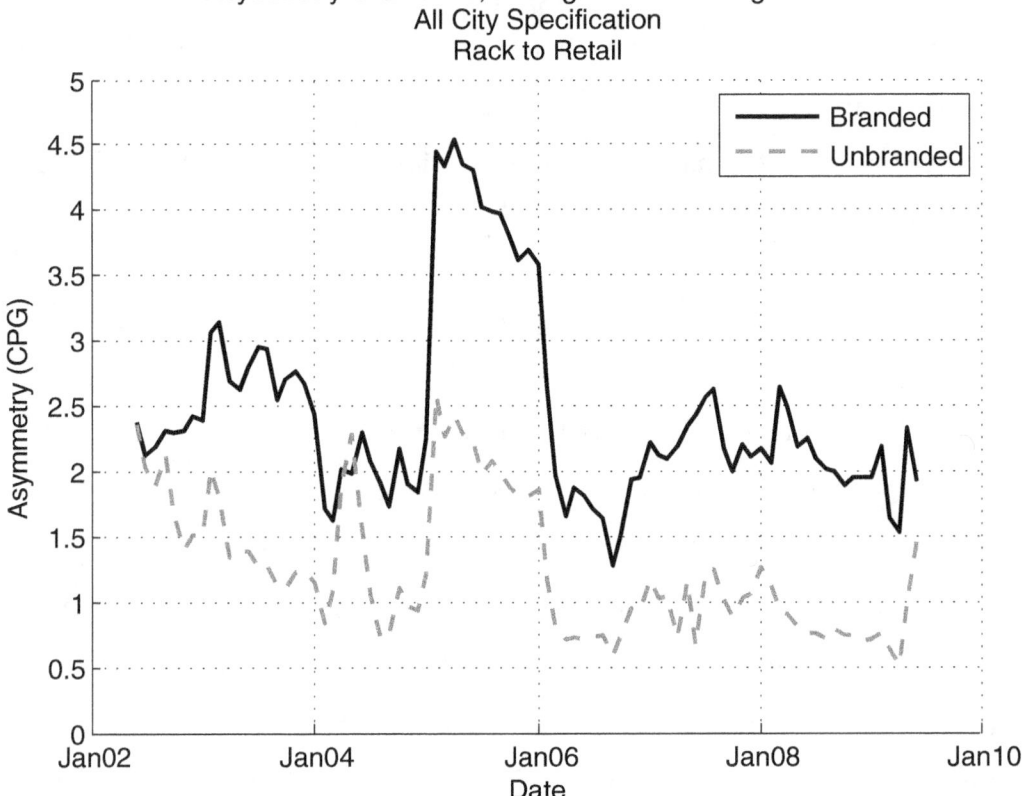

Figure 7: Time Analysis: Pass-Through Asymmetry by Year, National

4.6 Formal Tests of Asymmetry

In order to formally test for asymmetry, I report F-statistics for the pattern asymmetry in equation 6. I test the following hypothesis:

$$H_0: \quad \beta_{1i}^+ = \beta_{1i}^- \; \forall \; i$$

$$H_1: \quad \beta_{1i}^+ \neq \beta_{1i}^- \; \text{for some } i.$$

Note this is a two-sided test, so includes the possibility that the asymmetry is both the rockets and feather type and the opposite. To implement the test, I save the residual sum of squares, RSS_u, from the full (unrestricted) model where the coefficients are allowed to vary separately for positive and negative shocks. I then estimate a symmetric (restricted)

27

model, with only one set of β_{1i} coefficients and save RSS_r. Note that minimizing the BIC separately for each model would mean that a different number of lags is included in each.[21] Therefore, I again restrict the number of lags to be 14 days in both regressions so the only difference between the models is the restriction on the parameters. Formally, the test statistic is of the usual form:

$$\tilde{F} = \frac{(RSS_r - RSS_u)/(K_u - K_r)}{RSS_u/(N - K_u)},\tag{9}$$

where K_u and K_r are the number of parameters to be estimated in the unrestricted and restricted models respectively. Results are reported in tables 7, 8, and 9 below.

The statistics reported in the tables largely confirm what has been shown in the impulse response functions in the previous sections. There is strong evidence of asymmetry, both in each city separately and in the all-city specification, in rack to retail prices and spot to rack prices. The evidence is less strong when the upstream price is the crude oil price. The branded rack to retail price relationship again show stronger evidence of asymmetry compared with unbranded rack to retail prices.

The year-by-year regressions reveal some interesting patterns. Though the complete-year regressions show pattern asymmetry in San Francisco for branded rack to retail prices, the F-statistics for the individual year regressions are almost never significant. The branded rack to retail regressions for 2009 alone only show evidence of asymmetry in 17 of the 27 metro areas, though the complete-year regressions show strong asymmetry in 26 of the 27 metro areas. Thus, one implication is that studies which rely on shorter samples may not find evidence of asymmetry, when it does exist. Further investigation is required to determine what types of shocks (day-to-day movements versus large changes) are driving the asymmetric results over the entire sample.

---

[21]See Ye, et. al. (2005) for a discussion of this issue.

	WTI to Branded Rack	WTI to Unbranded Rack	WTI to Retail	Spot to Branded Rack	Spot to Unbranded Rack	Branded Rack to Retail	Unbranded Rack to Retail
Atlanta	3.33***	4.45***	2.00***	2.67***	12.53***	21.35***	17.74***
Boston	3.63***	3.69***	2.18***	5.34***	4.45***	16.08***	12.45***
Chicago	2.78***	2.66***	1.82**	16.83***	14.20***	8.47***	6.52***
Cleveland	3.36***	4.05***	1.58**	2.43***	3.84***	7.63***	6.72***
Dallas	5.39***	3.68***	3.10***	16.79***	18.73***	15.54***	12.05***
Denver	2.52***	3.01***	1.16	10.18***	6.44***	8.33***	6.29***
Detroit	3.36***	1.83**	1.77**	4.37***	4.46***	24.57***	15.28***
Washington DC	4.22***	4.63***	1.78**	16.43***	21.34***	15.49***	13.21***
Washington MD	4.22***	4.63***	3.26***	16.43***	21.34***	18.71***	15.42***
Washington VA	4.22***	4.63***	1.55*	16.43***	21.34***	21.98***	20.22***
Washington WV	4.10***	4.50***	1.58**	3.49***	3.77***	3.32***	5.54***
Houston	4.89***	5.23***	2.53***	17.31***	10.04***	24.12***	12.32***
Los Angeles	3.87***	2.35***	1.05	0.76	2.76***	9.34***	1.81**
Louisville IN	4.52***	4.09***	1.35	4.21***	1.86**	7.60***	6.69***
Louisville KY	3.73***	4.24***	2.08***	19.47***	20.61***	5.64***	6.92***
Miami	3.91***	3.28***	2.07***	1.81**	11.96***	19.75***	10.55***
Minneapolis St Paul MN	2.76***	3.67***	1.41	10.02***	3.88***	9.91***	9.18***
Minneapolis St Paul WI	2.76***	3.67***	4.80***	10.02***	3.88***	7.54***	6.38***
New Orleans	5.88***	4.25***	2.19***	3.48***	7.59***	11.35***	4.77***
Newark	3.32***	3.04***	3.14***	4.71***	2.93***	24.87***	14.91***
New York	3.32***	3.04***	2.60***	4.71***	2.93***	13.13***	7.70***
Phoenix	1.53*	3.79***	1.43*	2.21***	1.78**	3.84***	3.67***
Salt Lake City	3.56***	3.88***	1.35	1.68**	1.11	11.81***	7.20***
San Francisco	2.72***	2.11***	0.81	1.19	2.07***	3.75***	0.99
Seattle	3.70***	3.10***	1.06	2.65***	3.06***	10.25***	4.07***
St Louis IL	3.97***	2.33***	1.49*	4.86***	4.32***	6.36***	6.47***
St Louis MO	3.05***	6.33***	1.43*	16.08***	14.56***	7.41***	5.73***
All City Regression	69.58***	54.68***	240.65***	193.75***	192.97***	155.39***	86.97***

Significance at the 1% (***), 5% (**), and 10% (**) levels.

Table 7: F-Statistics On the Existence of Pattern Asymmetry (All Years)

5 Conclusion and Future Work

The purpose of this study was to understand why so many researchers have studied asymmetric pass-through in the gasoline industry and have come to varying conclusions. Many of the discrepancies can be explained by variations in the data and the model specification. I found that pass-through asymmetries do exist in wholesale rack to retail prices as well as in spot to retail prices, but the asymmetry is weak to non-existent in other price relationships.[22] Pass-through asymmetry in the branded wholesale to retail price relationship was shown to be larger than its unbranded counterpart. Averaging

---

[22]In some cases, I find evidence of prices rising *slower* than they fall, however the magnitude of this asymmetry is relatively small.

	2002	2003	2004	2005	2006	2007	2008	2009
Atlanta	1.50*	1.96***	1.70**	7.17***	1.33	2.14***	4.22***	2.02***
Boston	1.80**	5.07***	0.88	4.80***	1.55*	3.31***	1.55*	2.15***
Chicago	1.10	1.60**	1.56*	2.06***	1.41	3.13***	2.01***	2.11***
Cleveland	1.05	2.05***	2.56***	1.50*	1.17	1.92***	1.97***	1.80**
Dallas	2.72***	1.48*	2.08***	4.34***	1.70**	3.49***	2.53***	2.15***
Denver	1.28	1.30	1.06	3.83***	1.51*	1.42	0.95	1.83**
Detroit	0.82	1.04	3.39***	4.97***	3.43***	3.22***	4.49***	2.27***
Washington DC	0.49	1.11	1.08	5.47***	1.32	1.83**	2.65***	1.39
Washington MD	2.40***	1.73**	1.72**	5.29***	2.65***	2.20***	3.69***	2.01***
Washington VA	1.62**	1.64**	2.25***	6.16***	2.83***	2.97***	3.28***	2.25***
Washington WV	1.13	1.50*	1.27	2.74***	0.69	1.70**	1.30	1.82**
Houston	2.02***	2.21***	2.31***	7.18***	2.65***	5.54***	4.74***	3.79***
Los Angeles	1.40	2.30***	2.55***	1.69**	1.24	2.36***	2.34***	1.37
Louisville IN	1.69**	0.80	1.67**	3.32***	1.35	1.96***	2.01***	0.68
Louisville KY	0.82	0.76	1.33	3.03***	1.56*	1.47*	1.11	1.26
Miami	2.04***	2.31***	0.67	3.13***	4.76***	4.63***	2.38***	5.76***
Minneapolis St Paul MN	1.75**	0.71	2.53***	1.99***	2.92***	3.61***	2.08***	1.36
Minneapolis St Paul WI	2.06***	1.59**	2.50***	4.23***	2.14***	1.83**	1.19	1.13
New Orleans	1.49*	1.32	3.56***	2.06***	3.05***	3.07***	1.75**	2.70***
Newark	1.06	4.74***	1.09	6.33***	2.90***	2.16***	2.48***	2.28***
New York	0.85	3.70***	1.41	3.44***	1.68**	2.35***	1.44*	1.30
Phoenix	1.91***	1.67**	2.32***	2.46***	1.48*	1.05	0.96	0.82
Salt Lake City	1.79**	1.73**	1.70**	3.61***	4.18***	1.71**	2.68***	1.21
San Francisco	0.95	1.03	1.85**	1.05	1.54*	0.58	0.87	1.03
Seattle	2.27***	2.86***	2.83***	1.48*	0.79	3.95***	4.30***	2.10***
St Louis IL	1.78**	0.93	1.00	2.77***	1.10	1.47*	2.07***	1.20
St Louis MO	1.86**	1.51*	0.68	2.66***	1.69**	1.33	1.69**	1.93***
All City Regression	4.77***	7.71***	13.81***	47.00***	14.25***	16.00***	27.08***	10.57***

Significance at the 1% (***), 5% (**), and 10% (**) levels.

Table 8: F-Statistics, Branded Rack to Retail Prices (By Year)

daily data to obtain a weekly price series attenuates the findings of asymmetry as it masks important day-to-day variation in prices.

Still, this leaves several open questions including why there are differences in the pass-through asymmetry across cities and between branded and unbranded wholesale gasoline. Research that has attempted to explain the asymmetry has focused on the demand side, with consumer search cost and inventory management by drivers being the leading explanations. Unless consumers vary across cities, supply-side factors could help explain the geographic variation.

In future work, I will focus on which supply-side characteristics are associated with

	2002	2003	2004	2005	2006	2007	2008	2009
Atlanta	0.96	1.68**	1.07	3.06***	1.04	1.93***	2.71***	1.80**
Boston	0.89	4.03***	0.83	3.27***	1.45*	1.63**	1.48*	1.99***
Chicago	1.13	1.56*	1.32	2.43***	0.85	3.16***	2.01***	1.53*
Cleveland	0.84	1.78**	2.91***	2.18***	1.52*	1.42*	1.92***	1.31
Dallas	2.41***	1.12	1.67**	3.72***	1.65**	2.36***	1.54*	2.14***
Denver	1.30	0.60	1.36	4.14***	1.14	1.65**	1.57**	1.31
Detroit	0.72	1.55*	2.18***	3.94***	2.84***	1.67**	3.05***	0.80
Washington DC	0.67	1.14	1.15	6.08***	0.66	1.64**	0.87	1.50*
Washington MD	1.55*	0.95	1.44*	5.59***	1.58**	1.42	1.63**	1.80**
Washington VA	1.14	0.83	2.09***	11.14***	2.40***	1.74**	1.83**	1.67**
Washington WV	1.28	1.20	1.85**	4.14***	1.00	0.73	1.02	1.51*
Houston	2.74***	0.91	1.97***	3.89***	2.02***	1.94***	3.35***	2.16***
Los Angeles	1.08	1.27	1.42*	1.43*	1.11	1.08	2.07***	1.31
Louisville IN	1.25	0.98	2.54***	5.51***	1.31	1.19	1.27	1.08
Louisville KY	1.78**	0.63	1.44*	4.13***	1.57**	1.38	1.20	2.14***
Miami	2.29***	1.84**	0.50	1.74**	3.61***	2.52***	0.94	3.77***
Minneapolis St Paul MN	1.58**	0.45	1.90***	1.78**	2.47***	3.24***	2.12***	1.00
Minneapolis St Paul WI	1.61**	1.99***	1.85**	1.78**	1.70**	1.09	1.15	1.18
New Orleans	1.28	1.13	2.98***	1.32	2.41***	2.18***	0.88	1.36
Newark	0.85	3.83***	0.70	3.39***	0.67	1.82**	2.60***	1.61**
New York	0.52	2.49***	1.00	3.70***	0.86	2.19***	1.00	1.21
Phoenix	1.64**	1.23	0.64	4.10***	1.76**	2.66***	1.26	1.73**
Salt Lake City	3.30***	1.03	0.86	4.10***	2.72***	2.06***	1.76**	0.92
San Francisco	0.89	1.33	0.99	0.52	0.78	0.42	0.81	0.53
Seattle	1.67**	2.01***	1.70**	0.83	1.54*	1.88***	1.38	1.11
St Louis IL	1.16	0.84	0.94	1.97***	1.32	1.72**	4.36***	1.33
St Louis MO	0.86	0.84	0.77	2.17***	2.20***	0.90	1.87**	2.28***
All City Regression	3.19***	4.66***	11.33***	33.01***	7.06***	8.48***	15.08***	5.30***

Significance at the 1% (***), 5% (**), and 10% (**) levels.

Table 9: F-Statistics, Unbranded Rack to Retail Prices (By Year)

more or less asymmetric pass-through. These may include differences in the retail ownership structure (e.g., a larger percentage of lessee-dealer owned stations versus independents) similar to the study by Lewis (2009) and retail concentration similar to the study by Deltas (2008). In addition, the results in this paper indicate that, at least in some cities, pass-through asymmetry varies over time. Supply-side shocks caused by hurricanes, pipeline disruptions, and refinery maintenance or outages, which only affect certain geographic areas and vary from year to year, may provide an explanation.

References

[1] Bachmeier, Lance and James Griffin, (2003). "New Evidence on Asymmetric Gasoline Price Responses." *The Review of Economics and Statistics,* 85(3), August 2003.

[2] Bacon, Robert W., (1991). "Rockets and Feathers: The Asymmetric Speed of Adjustment of UK Retail Gasoline Prices to Cost Changes." *Energy Economics,* 13 July 1991.

[3] Borenstein, S., C. A. Cameron and R. Gilbert, (1997). "Do Gasoline Prices Respond Asymmetrically to Crude Oil Price Changes?" *Quarterly Journal of Economics,* 112(1), 1997.

[4] Borenstein, S., (1991). "Selling Costs and Switching Costs: Explaining Retail Gasoline Margins." *The RAND Journal of Economics,* 22(3), 1991.

[5] Borenstein, S., Andrea Shepard (1996). "Dynamic Pricing in Retail Gasoline Markets." *The RAND Journal of Economics,* 27(3), 1996.

[6] Bulow, Jeremy and Paul Pfleiderer, (1983). "A Note on the Effect of Cost Changes on Prices." *Journal of Political Economy,* 91, 1983.

[7] Deltas, George (2008). "Retail Gasoline Price Dynamics and Local Market Power." *The Journal of Industrial Economics,* 61(3), September 2008.

[8] Eckert, Andrew (2002). "Retail Price Cycles and Response Asymmetry." *Canadian Journal of Economics,* 35(1), 2002.

[9] Energy Information Administration, US Department of Energy, (2007). "Refinery Outages: Description and Potential Impact on Petroleum Product Prices." March 2007.

[10] Energy Information Administration, US Department of Energy, (2008). "A Primer on Gasoline Prices." Online: `http://www.eia.doe.gov/bookshelf/brochures/gasolinepricesprimer/index.html` [Downloaded: 09/11/2008], May 2008.

[11] Engle R. and C.W.J. Granger, (1987). "Co-Integration and Error Correction: Representation, Estimation, and Testing." *Econometrica,* 55(2), 1987.

[12] Espey, Molly, (1996). "Explaining Variation in Elasticity of Gasoline Demand in the United States: A Meta Analysis." *The Energy Journal,* 17, 1996.

[13] The Federal Trade Commission, (2006). "Investigation of Gasoline Price Manipulation and Post-Katrina Gasoline Price Increases." Spring 2006.

[14] The Federal Trade Commission, (2005). "Gasoline Price Changes: The Dynamics of Supply, Demand and Competition." Available at http://www.ftc.gov/reports/gasprices05/050705gaspricesrpt.pdf, 2005.

[15] Godby, R, A.M. Lintner, T. Stengos, and B. Wandschneider, (2000). "Testing for Asymmetric Pricing in the Canadian Retail Gasoline Market." *Energy Economics,* 22, 2000.

[16] Goldberg, Pinelopi K. and Rebecca Hellerstein, (2008). "A Structural Approach to Explaining Incomplete Exchange-Rate Pass-Through and Pricing-to-Market." *The American Economic Review,* 98(2), 2008.

[17] Goodwin, Barry, and Matthew Holt, (1999). "Price Transmission and Asymmetric Adjustment in the U.S. Beef Sector." *American Journal of Agricultural Economics,* 81, August 1999.

[18] The Government Accountability Office, (2006). "Energy Markets: Factors Contributing to Higher Gasoline Prices." GAO-06-412T. February 2006.

33

[19] Gron, Anne, Deborah Swenson, (2000). "Cost Pass-Through in the U.S. Automobile Market." *The Review of Economics and Statistics,* 82(2), 2000.

[20] Hastings, Justine, Jennifer Brown, Erin Mansur, and Sofia Villas-Boas, (2008). "Reformulating Competition? Gasoline Content Regulation and Wholesale Gasoline Prices." *Journal of Environmental Economics and Management,* January 2008.

[21] Hosken, Daniel, Robert McMillan and Christopher Taylor, (2008). "Retail Gasoline Pricing: What Do We Know?" *International Journal of Industrial Organization,* 26(6), November 2008.

[22] Kim, Donghun and Ronald Cotterill, (2008). "Cost Pass-Through in Differentiated Product Markets: The Case of U.S. Processed Cheese." *The Journal of Industrial Economics,* 60(1), March 2008.

[23] Knittel, Christopher, Jonathan E. Hughes, and Daniel Sperling, (2008). "Evidence of a Shift in the Short-Run Price Elasticity of Gasoline Demand." *The Energy Journal,* 29(1), January 2008.

[24] Lewis, Matt, (forthcoming). "Asymmetric Price Adjustment and Consumer Search: an Examination of Retail Gasoline Market," forthcoming in *Journal of Economics and Management Strategy.*

[25] Lewis, Matt, and Michael Noel (forthcoming). "The Speed of Gasoline Price Response in Markets with and without Edgeworth Cycles," forthcoming in *The Review of Economic Studies.*

[26] Lewis, Matt (2009). "Temporary Wholesale Gasoline Price Spikes have Long Lasting Retail Effects: The Aftermath of Hurricane Rita." *Journal of Law and Economics,* 52(3), 2009.

[27] Lidderdale, T.C.M. (United States Energy Information Administration), (1999). "Environmental Regulations and Changes in Petroleum Refining Operations." Online: `http://www.eia.doe.gov/emeu/steo/pub/special/enviro.html` [Downloaded: 12/07/2007], 1999.

[28] MacKinnon, James, (2010). "Critical Values for Cointegration Tests." Queen's Economics Department Working Paper No. 1227. 2010.

[29] Noel, Michael D., (2007). "Edgeworth Price Cycles, Cost-Based Pricing, and Sticky Pricing in Retail Gasoline Markets." *Review of Economics and Statistics,* Vol. 89, 2007.

[30] Peterson, D. J. and Sergej Mahnovski, (2003). "New Forces at Work in Refining: Industry Views of Critical Business and Operations Trends." Santa Monica, CA : RAND, 2003.

[31] The United States Senate, (2002). "Gas Prices: How are they Really Set?" Online: `http://www.senate.gov/~gov_affairs/042902gasreport.htm` [Downloaded 10/01/2007], May 2002.

[32] Ten Kate, Adriaan and Gunnar Niels, (2005). "To What Extent are Cost Savings Passed on to Consumers? An Oligopoly Approach." *European Journal of Law and Economics,* 20, 2005.

[33] Ye, Michael, John Zyren, Joanne Shore, and Michael Burdette, (2005). "Regional Comparisons, Spatial Aggregation, and Asymmetry of Price Pass-Through in U.S. Gasoline Markets." *Atlantic Economic Journal,* 33, 2005.

A   Appendix

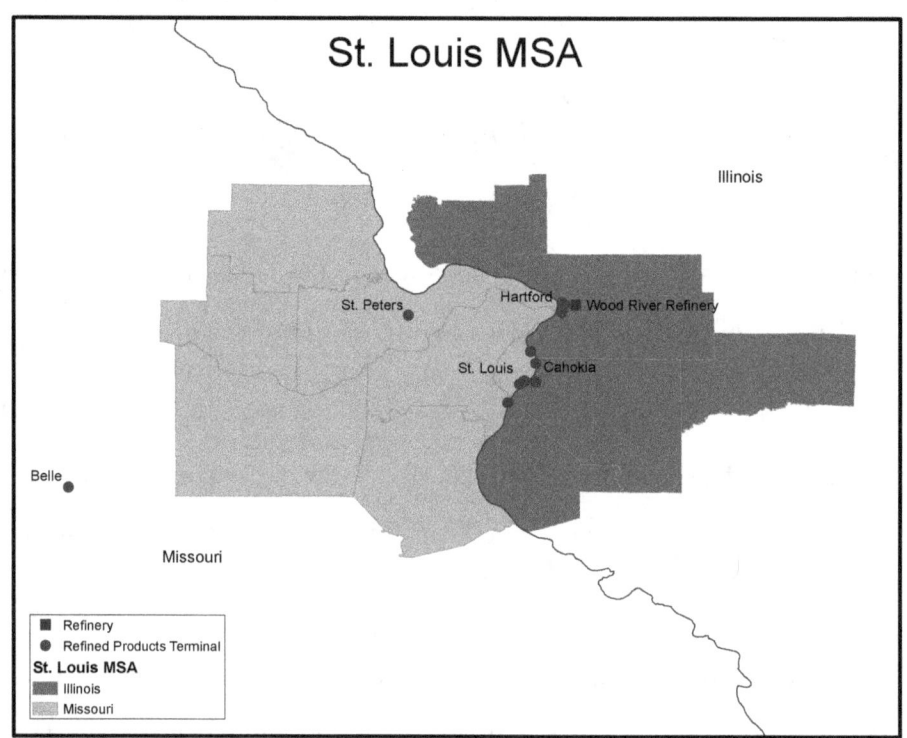

Figure A.1: St. Louis Retail Market Areas.

Parameter	Estimate	Standard Error
Constant	-0.087***	0.011
+ (Rack(t) - Rack(t-1))	0.274***	0.004
+ (Rack(t-1) - Rack(t-2))	0.101***	0.004
+ (Rack(t-2) - Rack(t-3))	0.059***	0.004
+ (Rack(t-3) - Rack(t-4))	0.036***	0.004
+ (Rack(t-4) - Rack(t-5))	0.052***	0.004
+ (Rack(t-5) - Rack(t-6))	0.044***	0.004
- (Rack(t) - Rack(t-1))	0.068***	0.004
- (Rack(t-1) - Rack(t-2))	0.085***	0.004
- (Rack(t-2) - Rack(t-3))	0.056***	0.004
- (Rack(t-3) - Rack(t-4))	0.075***	0.004
+ (Retail(t-1) - Retail(t-2))	0.335***	0.005
+ (Retail(t-2) - Retail(t-3))	-0.244***	0.005
- (Retail(t-1) - Retail(t-2))	0.328***	0.012
- (Retail(t-2) - Retail(t-3))	0.101***	0.013
- (Retail(t-3) - Retail(t-4))	-0.025**	0.012
- (Retail(t-4) - Retail(t-5))	0.011	0.012
- (Retail(t-5) - Retail(t-6))	0.132***	0.011
+ EC Term	-0.021***	0.001
- EC Term	-0.059***	0.002
N		54,530
R^2		0.45
Durbin-Watson Statistic		2.020

*Dependent Variable: Retail(t) - Retail(t-1). City-level fixed effects included in the first-stage regression. ***, **, * significant at the 1%, 5% and 10% levels respectively.*

Table A.1: Regression Results: Branded Rack to Retail Prices, All Cities Included

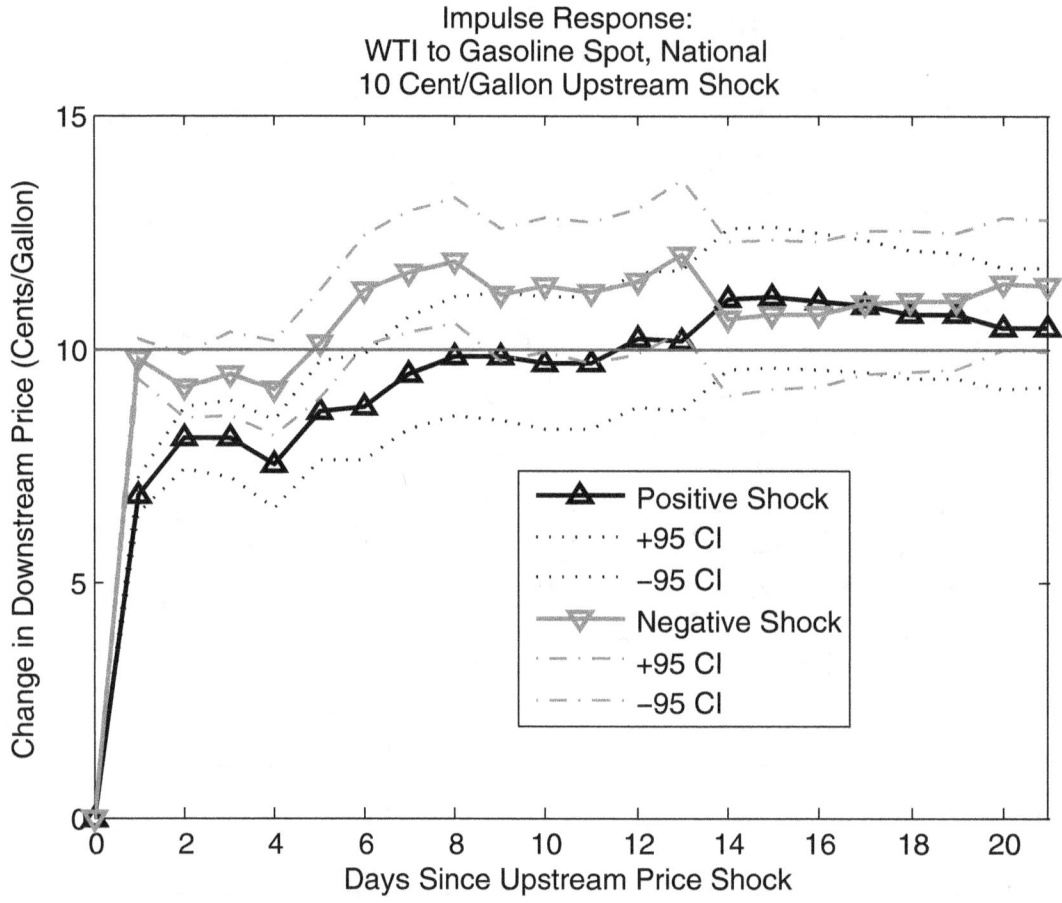

Figure A.2: Impulse Response Function: Crude Oil to Gasoline Spot Prices, All Cities Included

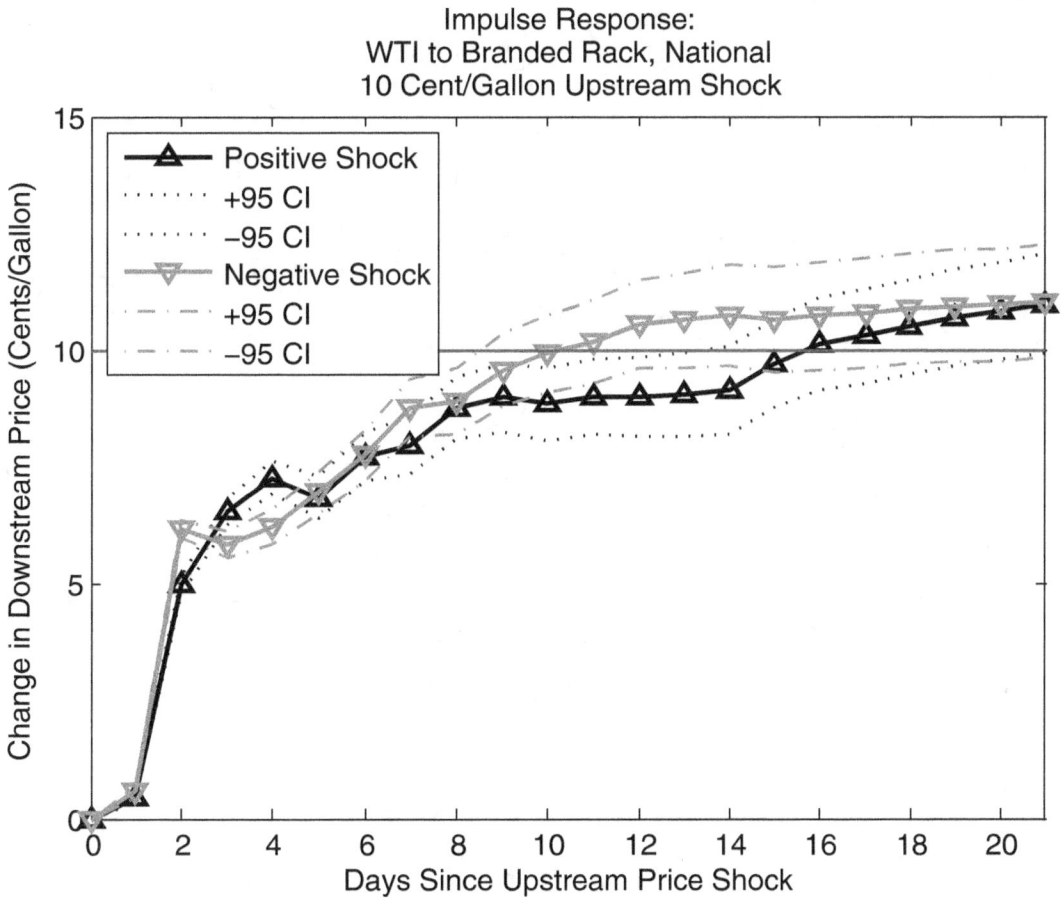

Figure A.3: Impulse Response Function: Crude Oil to Rack Prices, All Cities Included

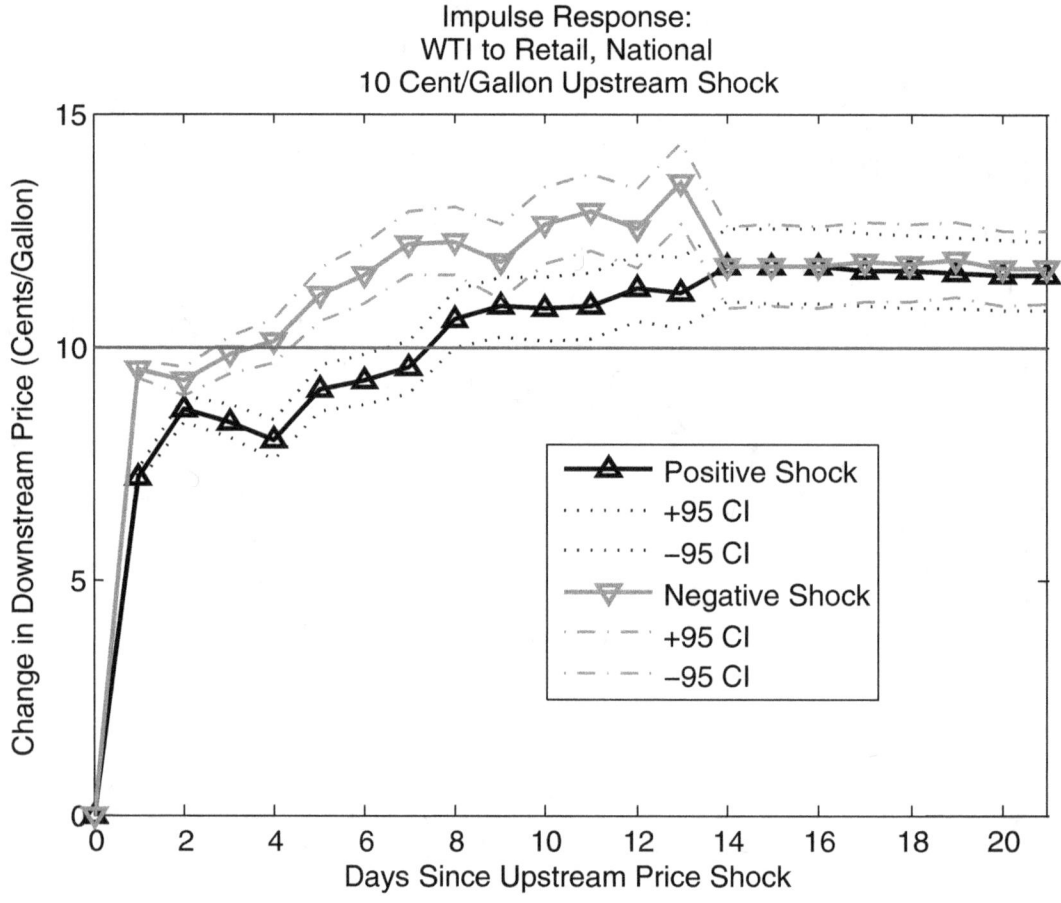

Figure A.4: Impulse Response Function: Crude Oil to Retail Prices, All Cities Included

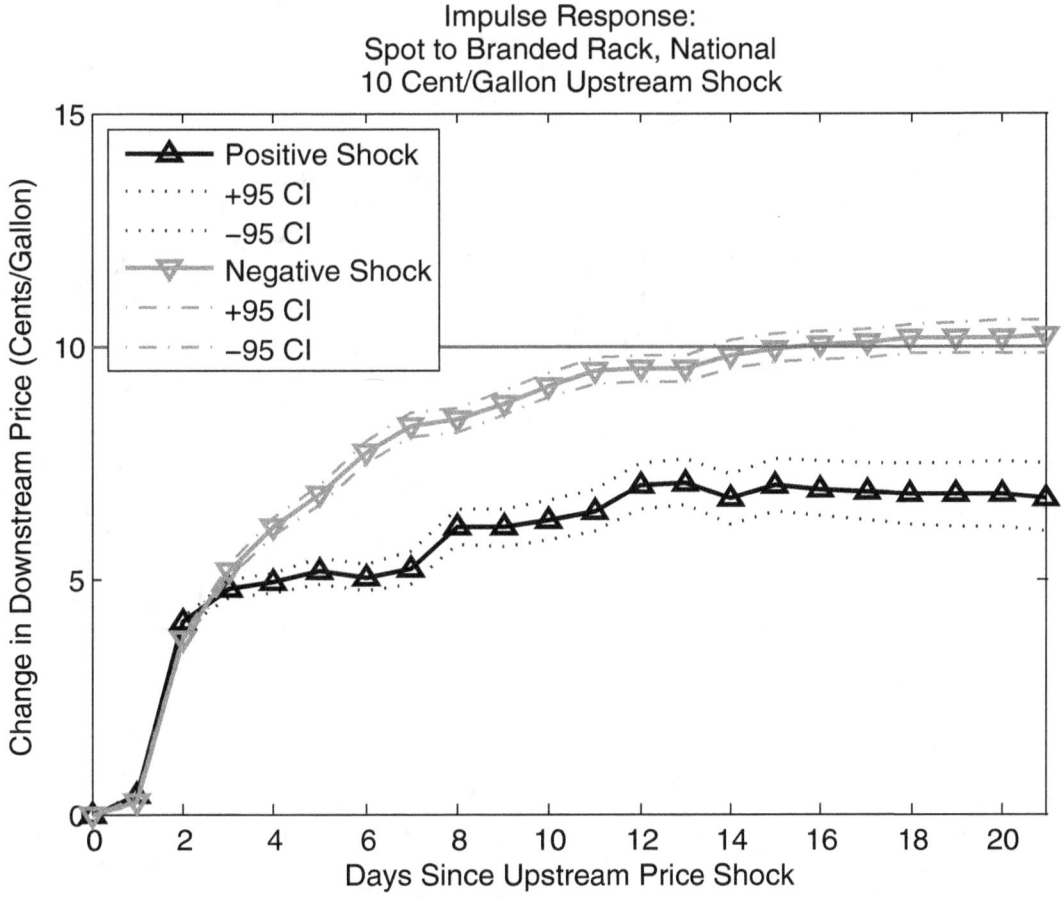

Figure A.5: Impulse Response Function: Gasoline Spot to Rack, All Cities Included

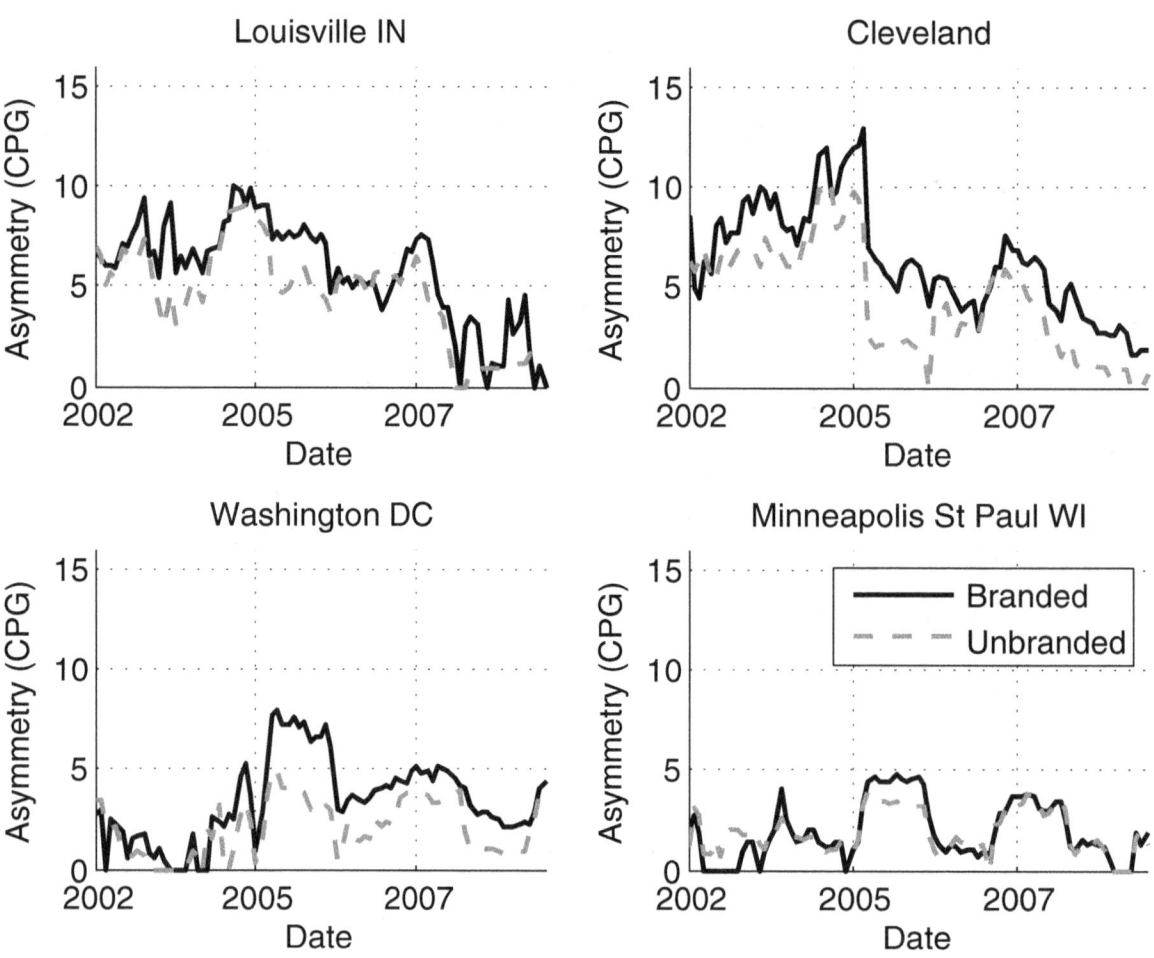

Figure A.6: Time Analysis: Pass-Through Asymmetry over Time and by City